Swear Word Coloring Book

MAGICAL BEASTS & UNICORNS
SWEAR WORD COLORING BOOK

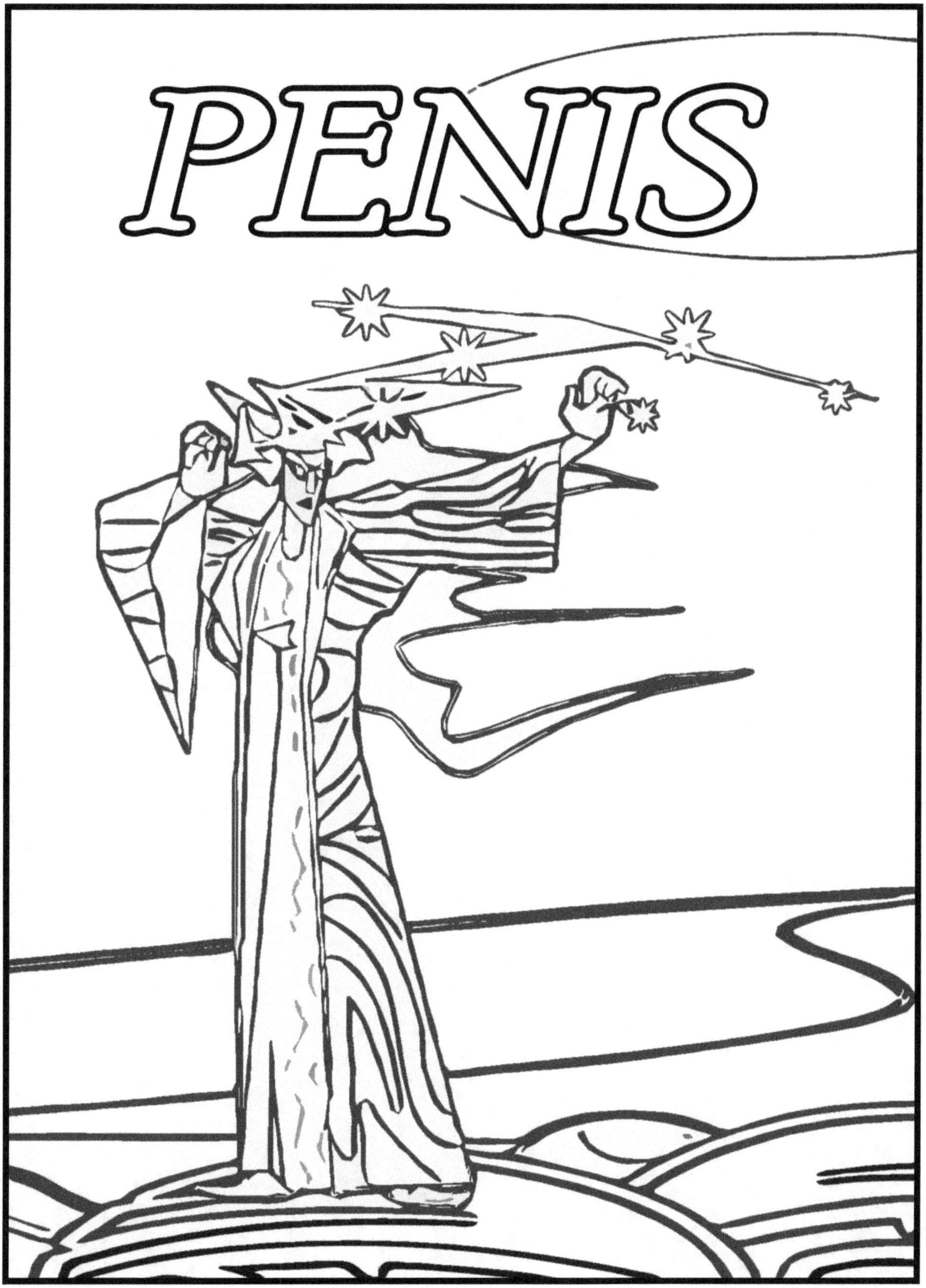
PENIS

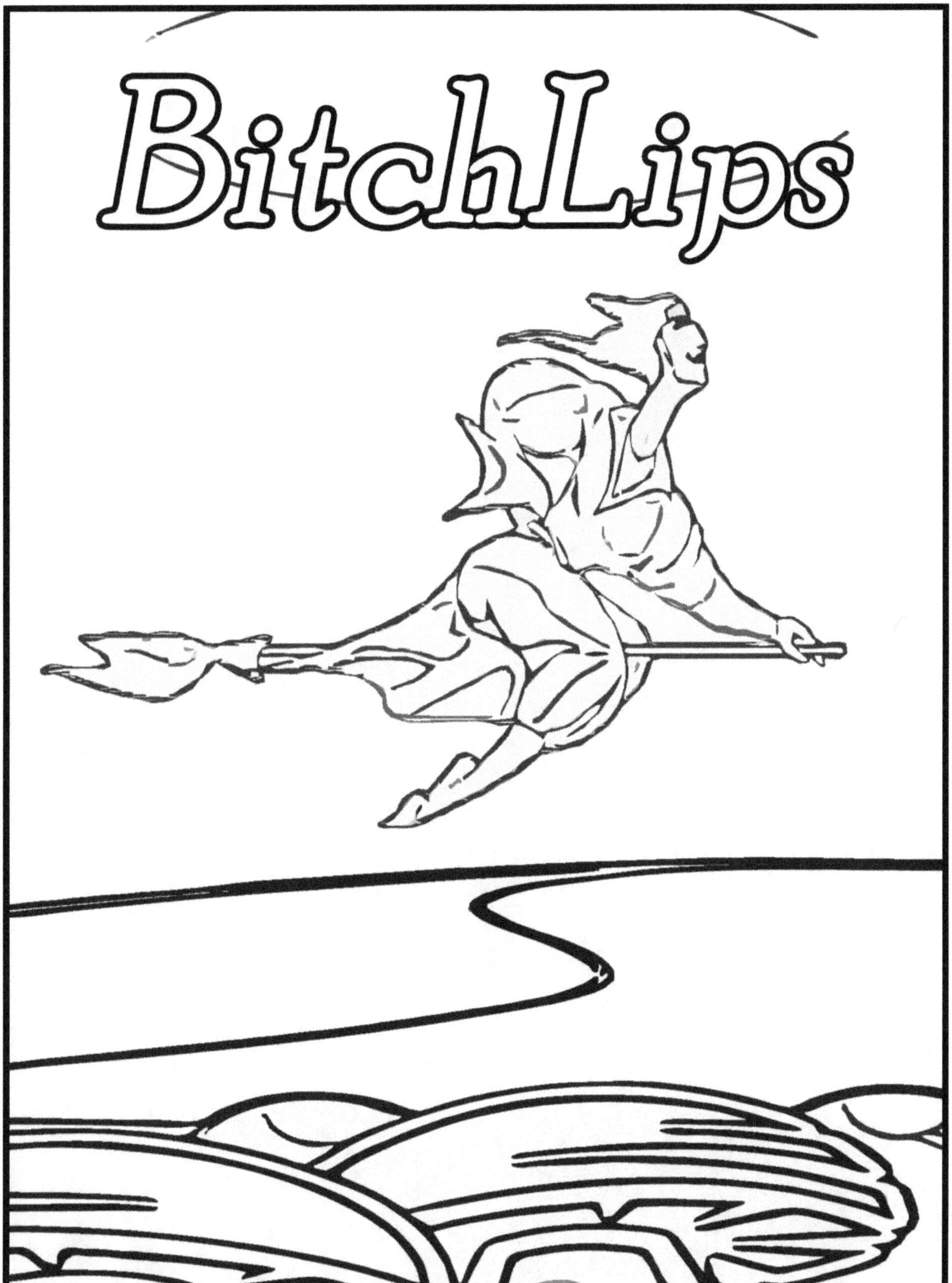
BitchLips

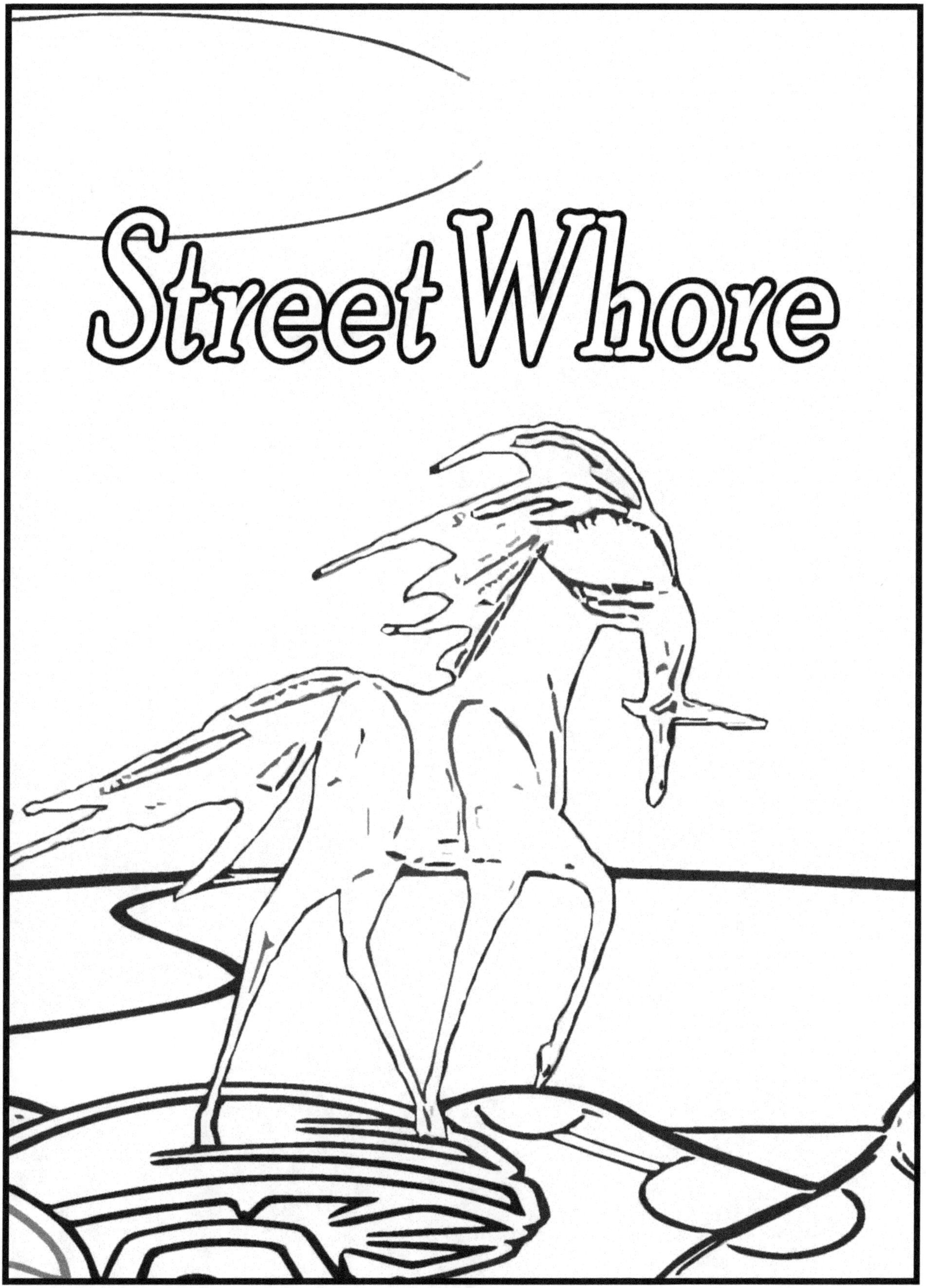
Street Whore

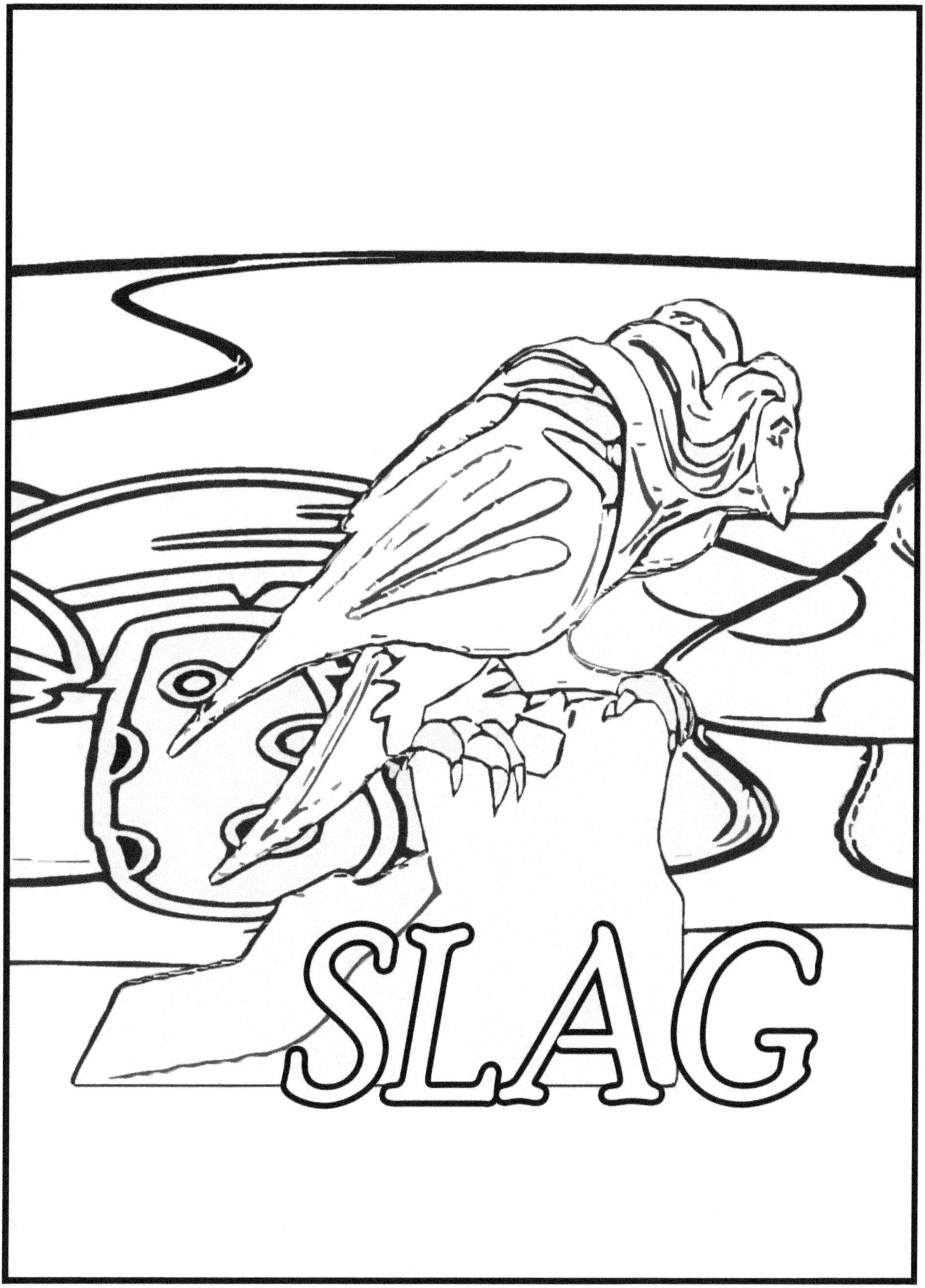
SLAG

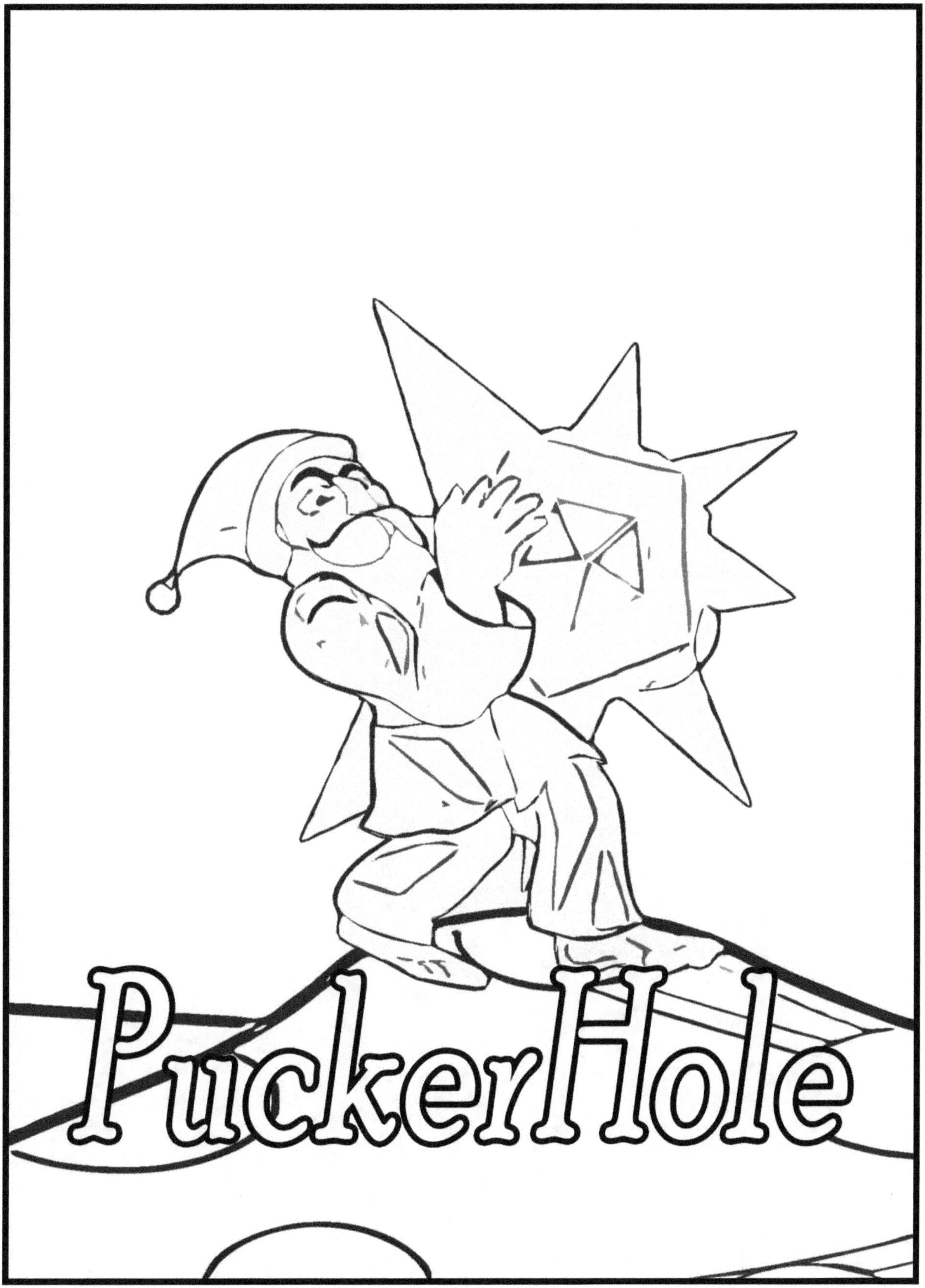
PuckerHole

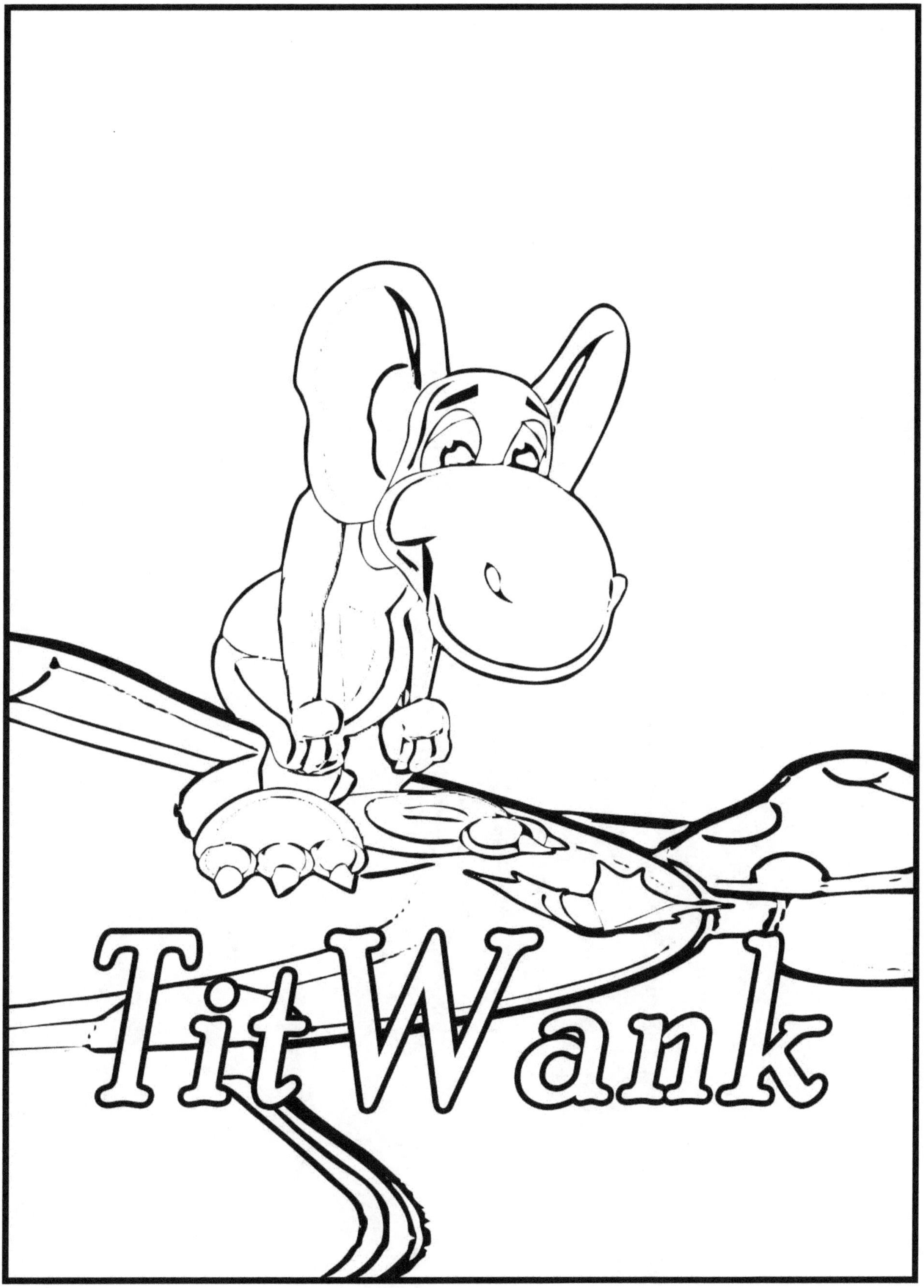
Tit Wank

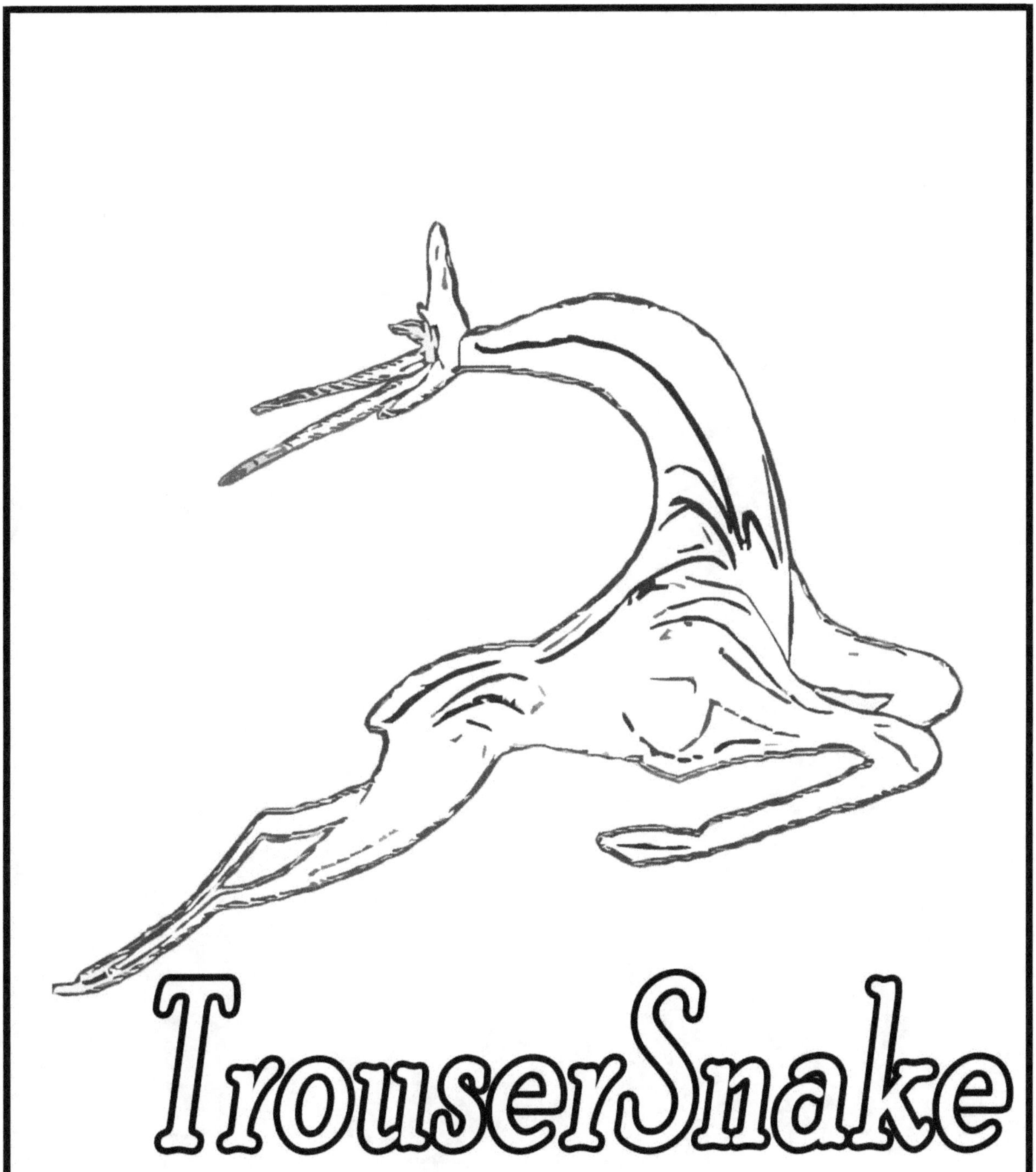
TrouserSnake

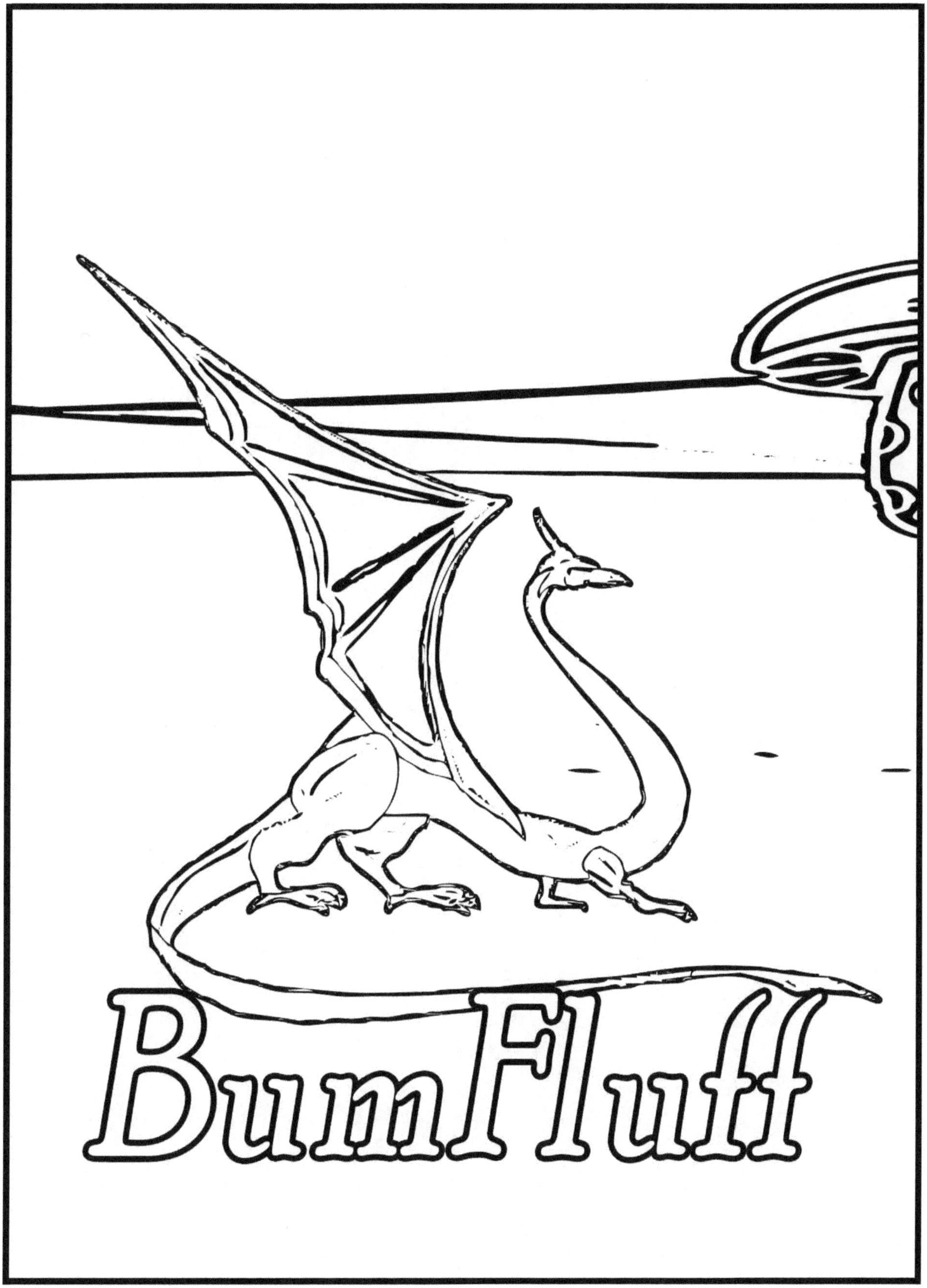
BumFluff

Cockface

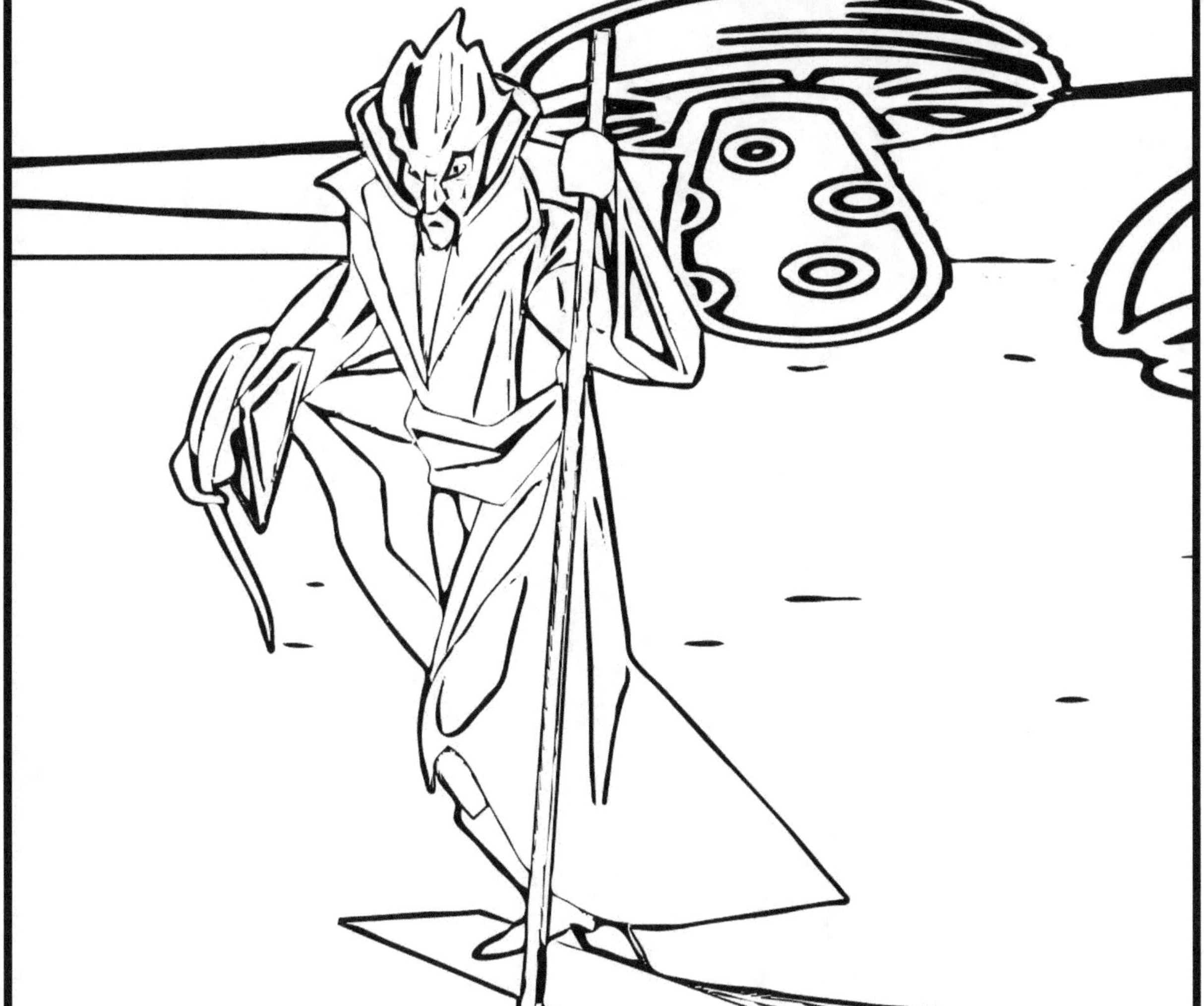

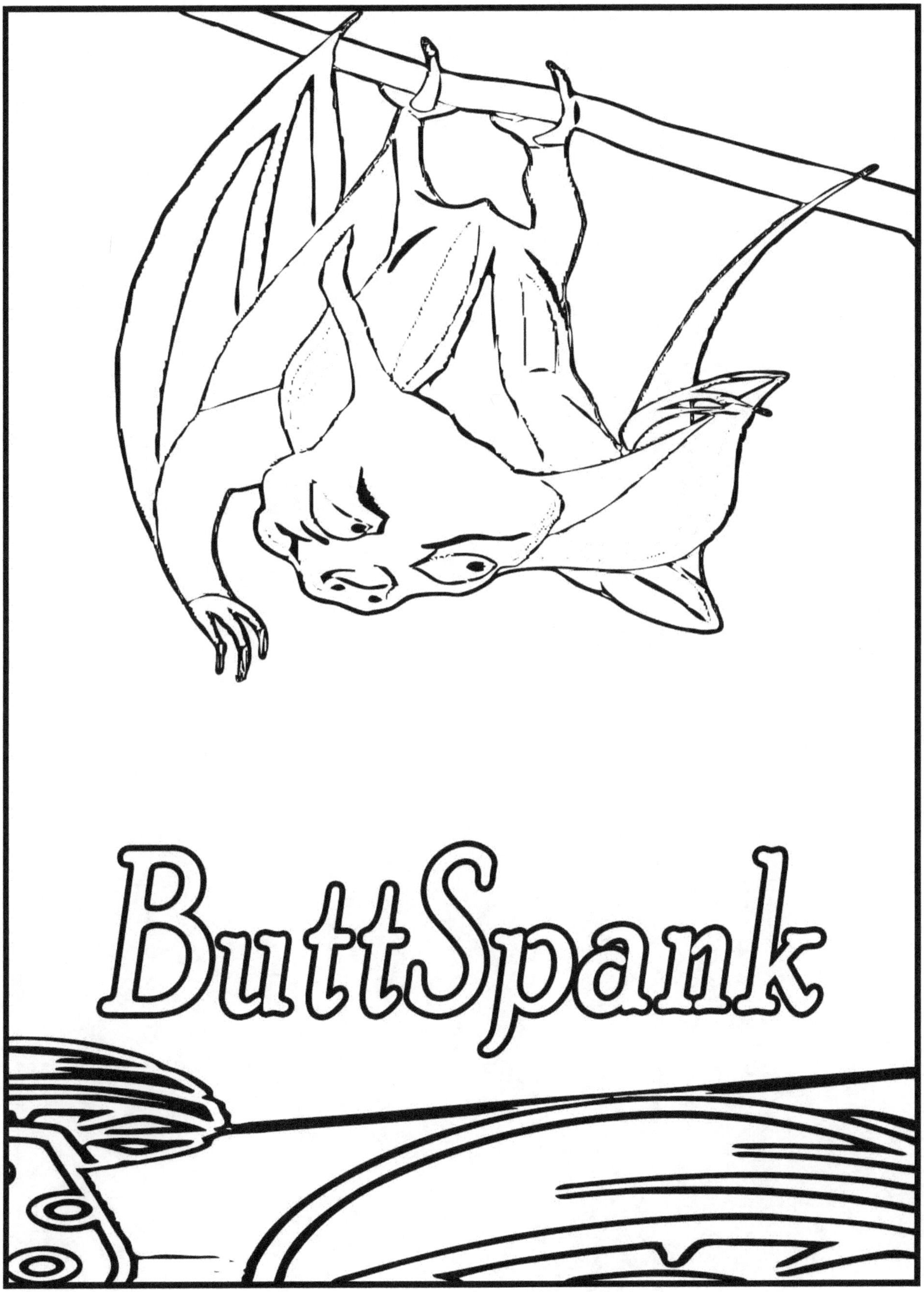
ButtSpank

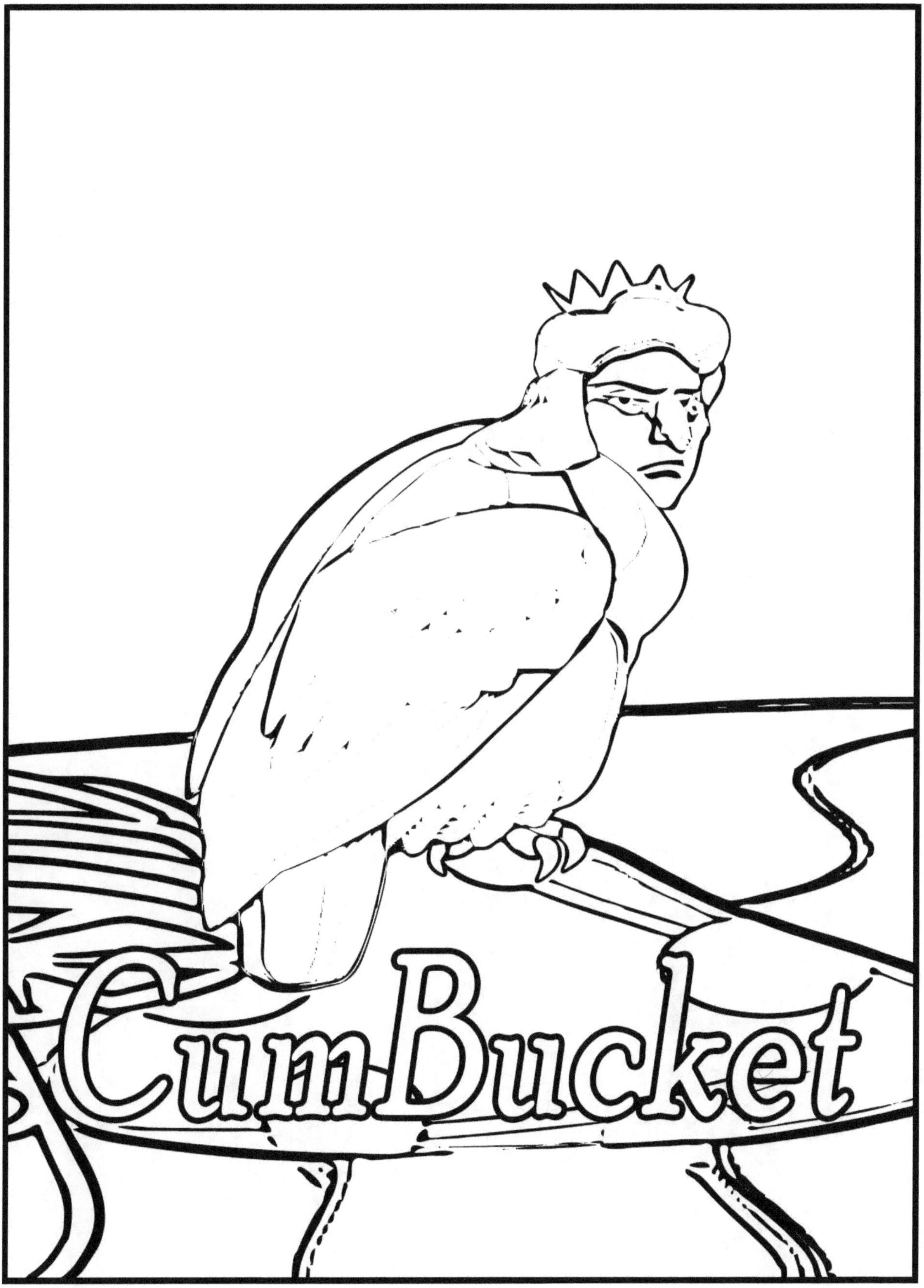
CumBucket

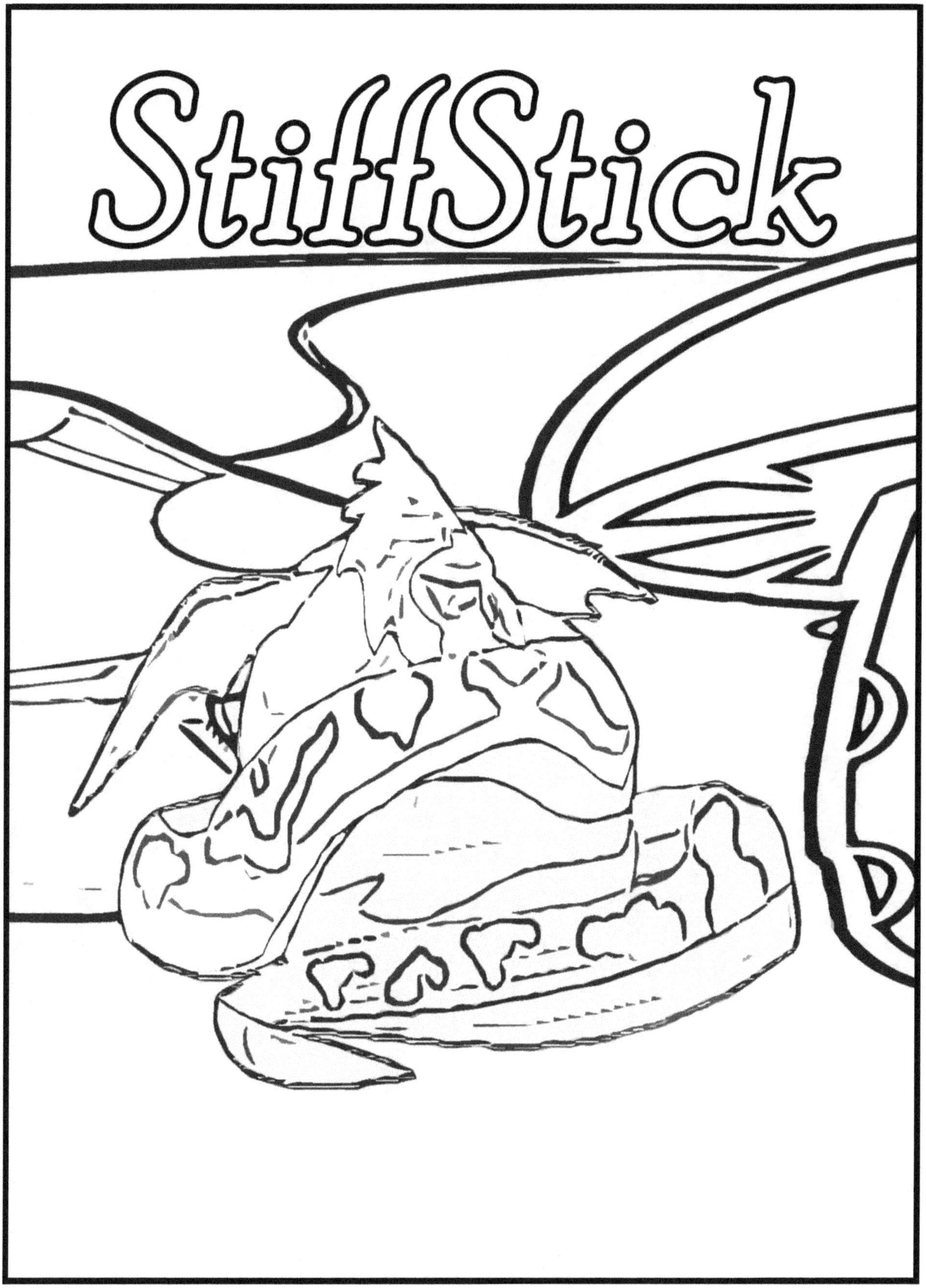
StiffStick

MuffDiver

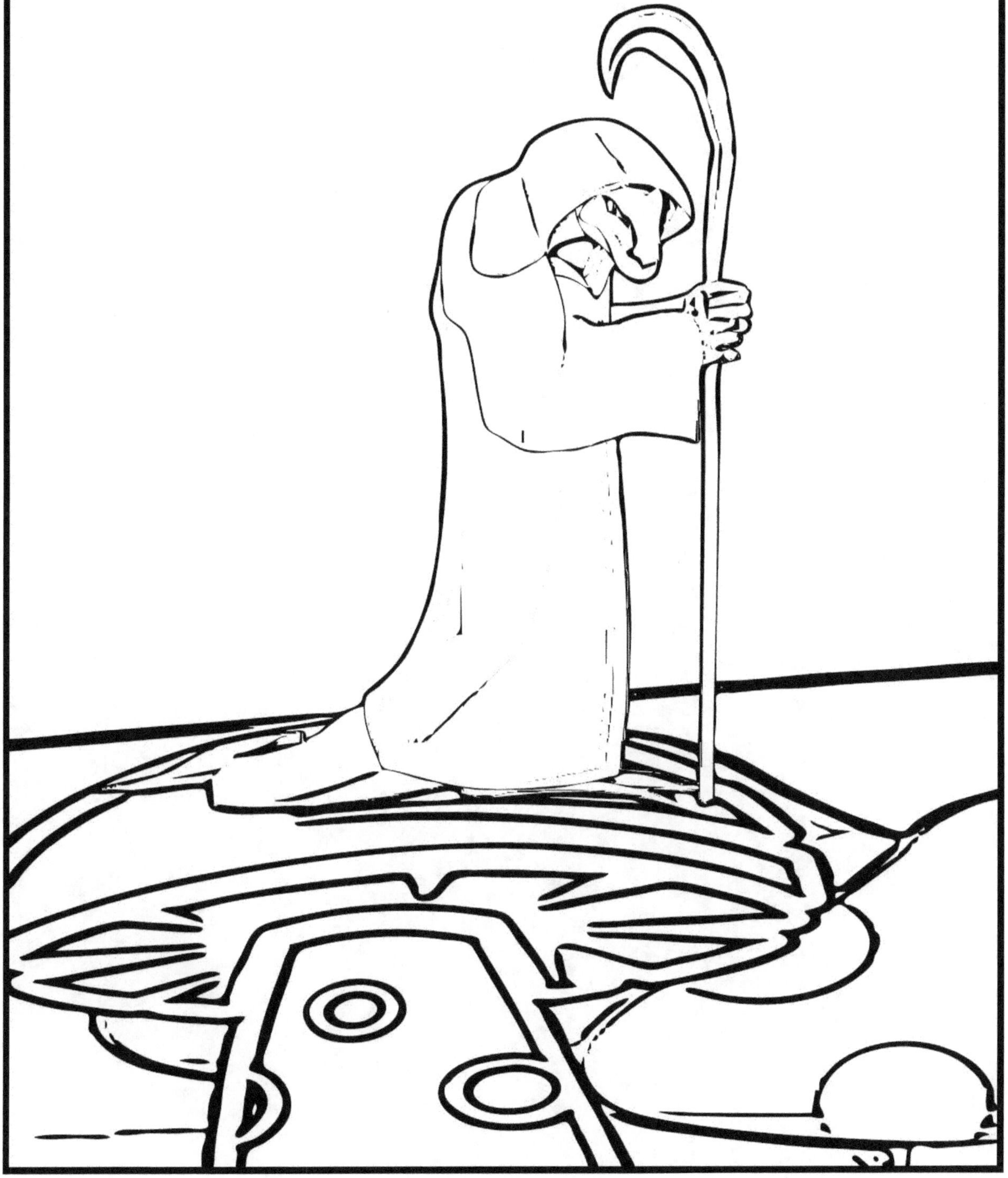

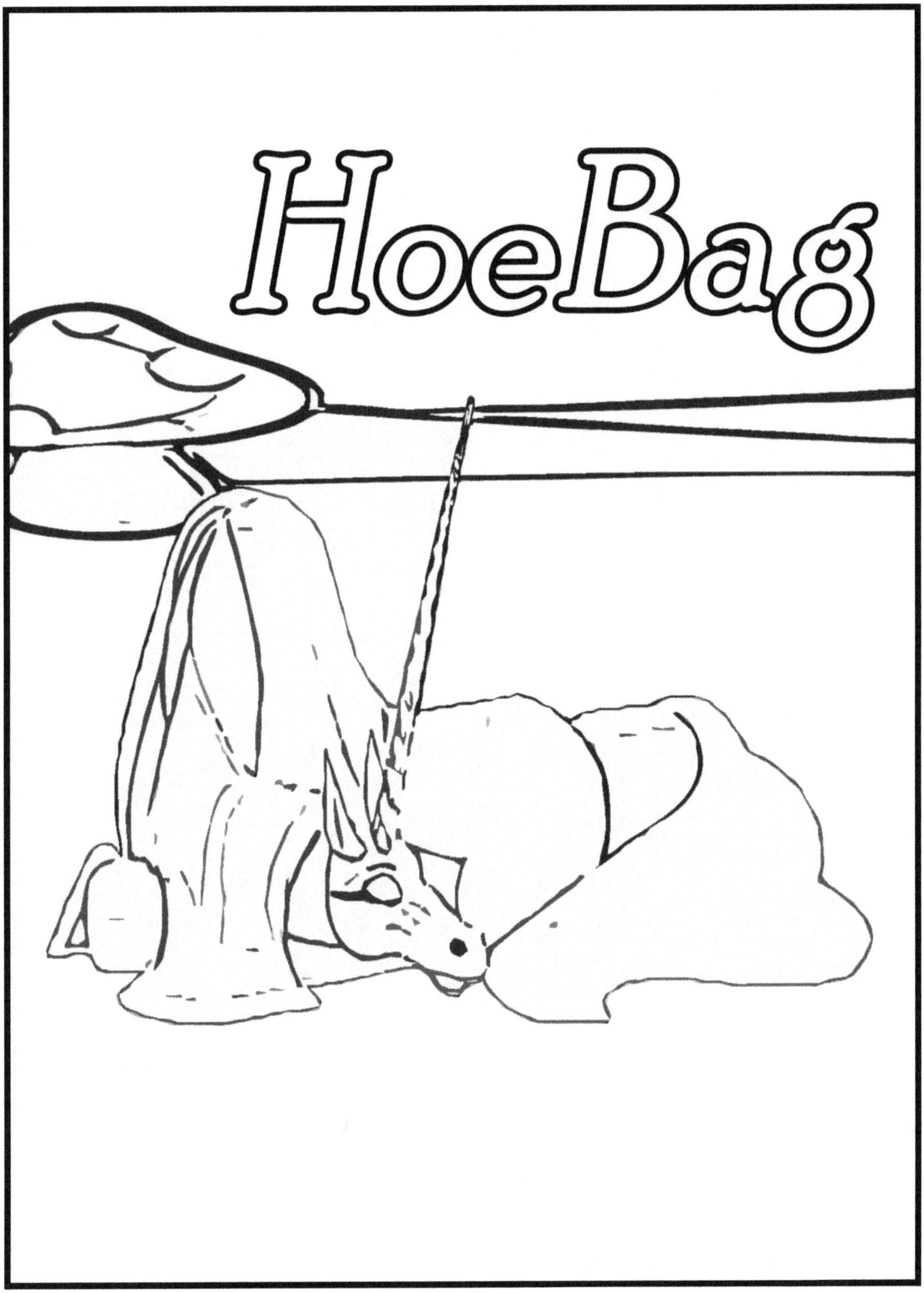
HoeBag

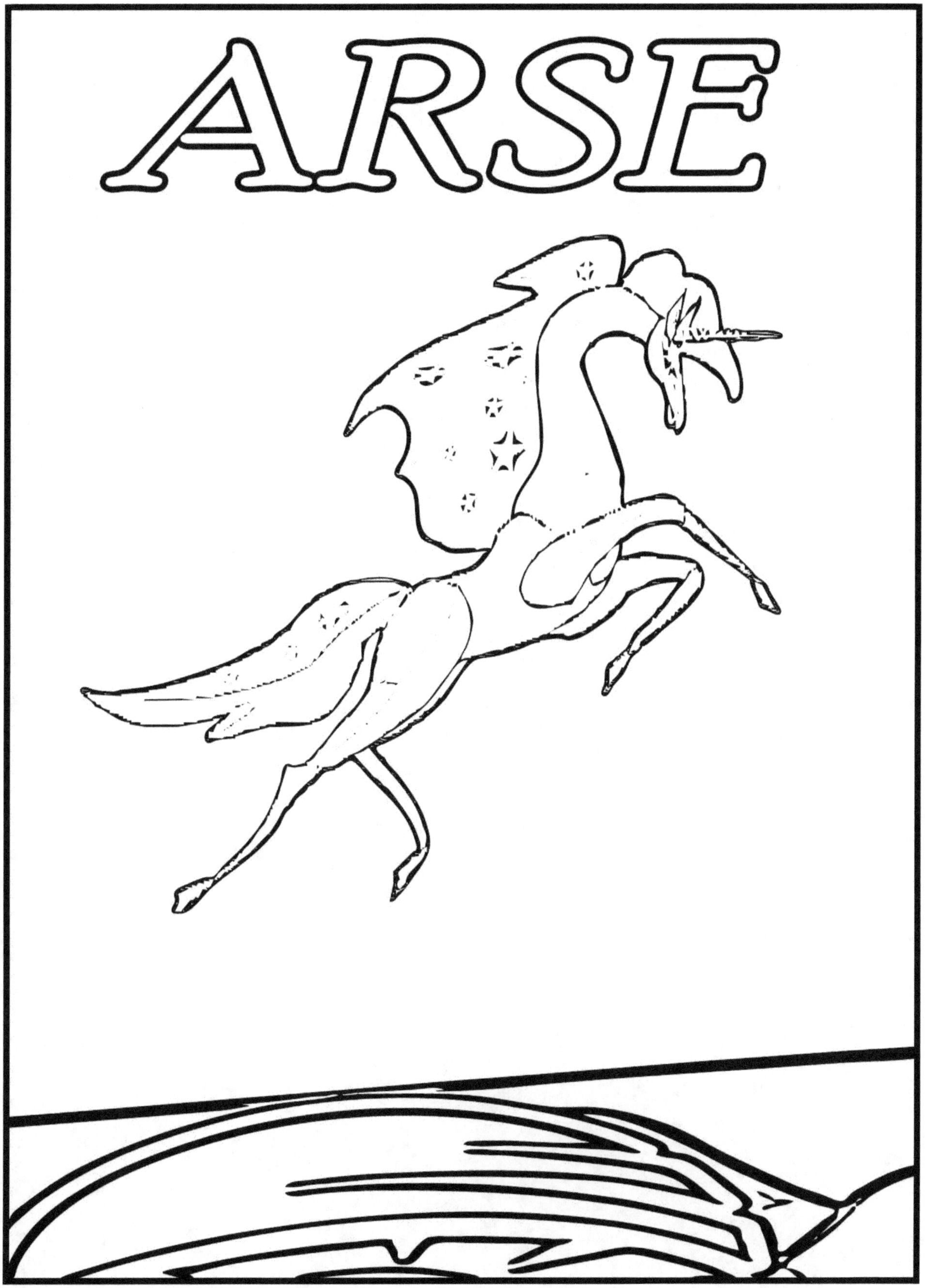
ARSE

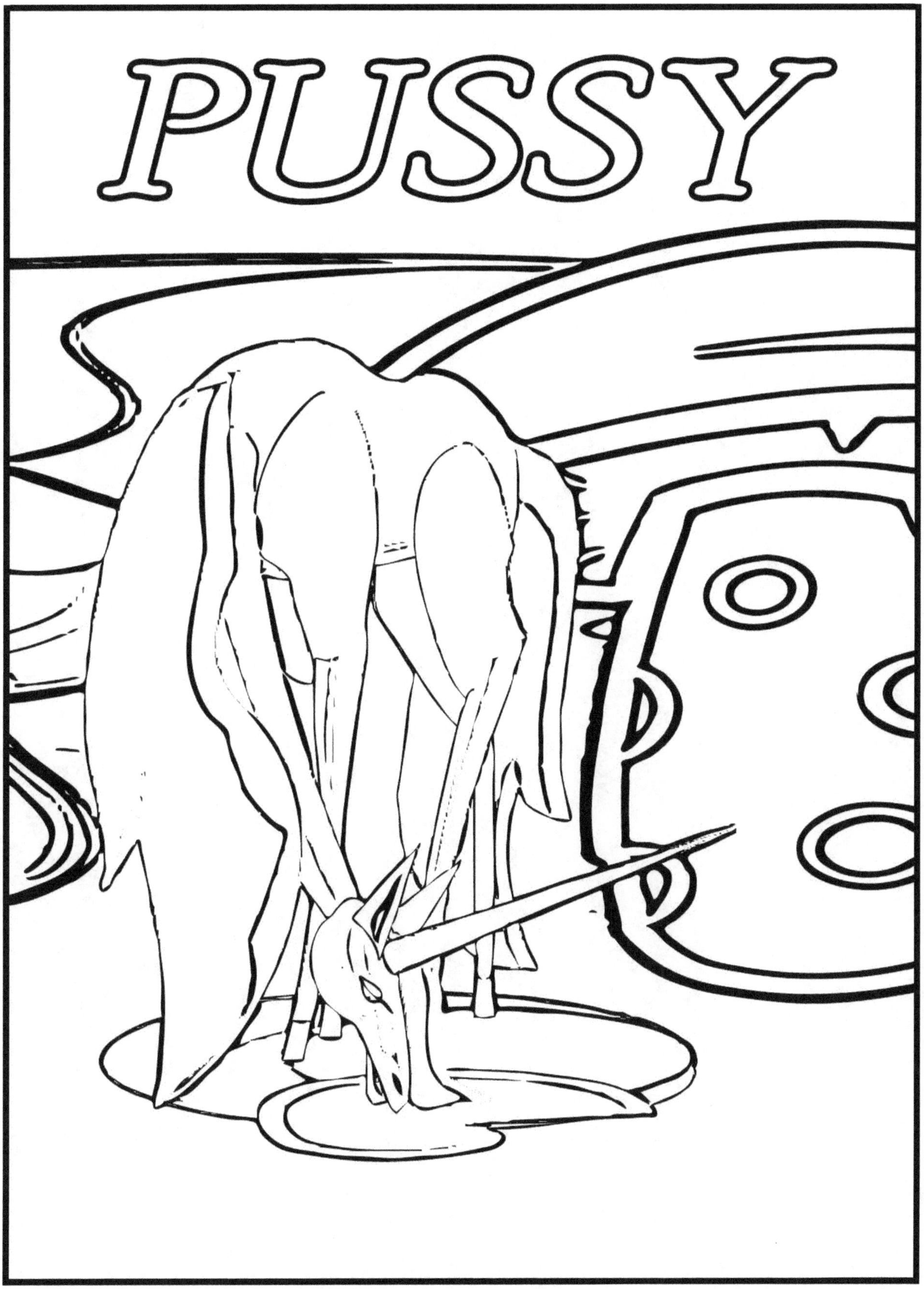
PUSSY

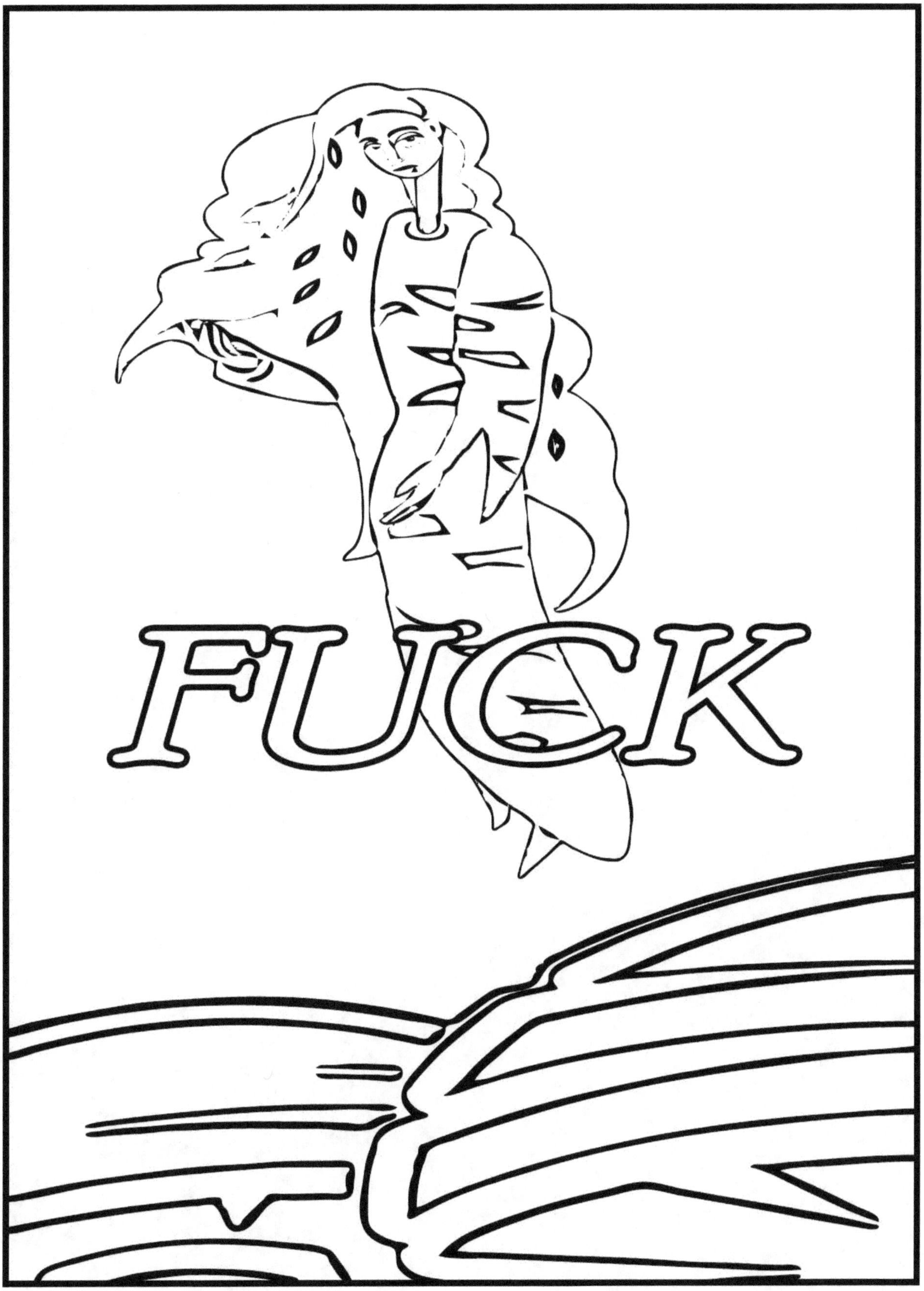
FUCK

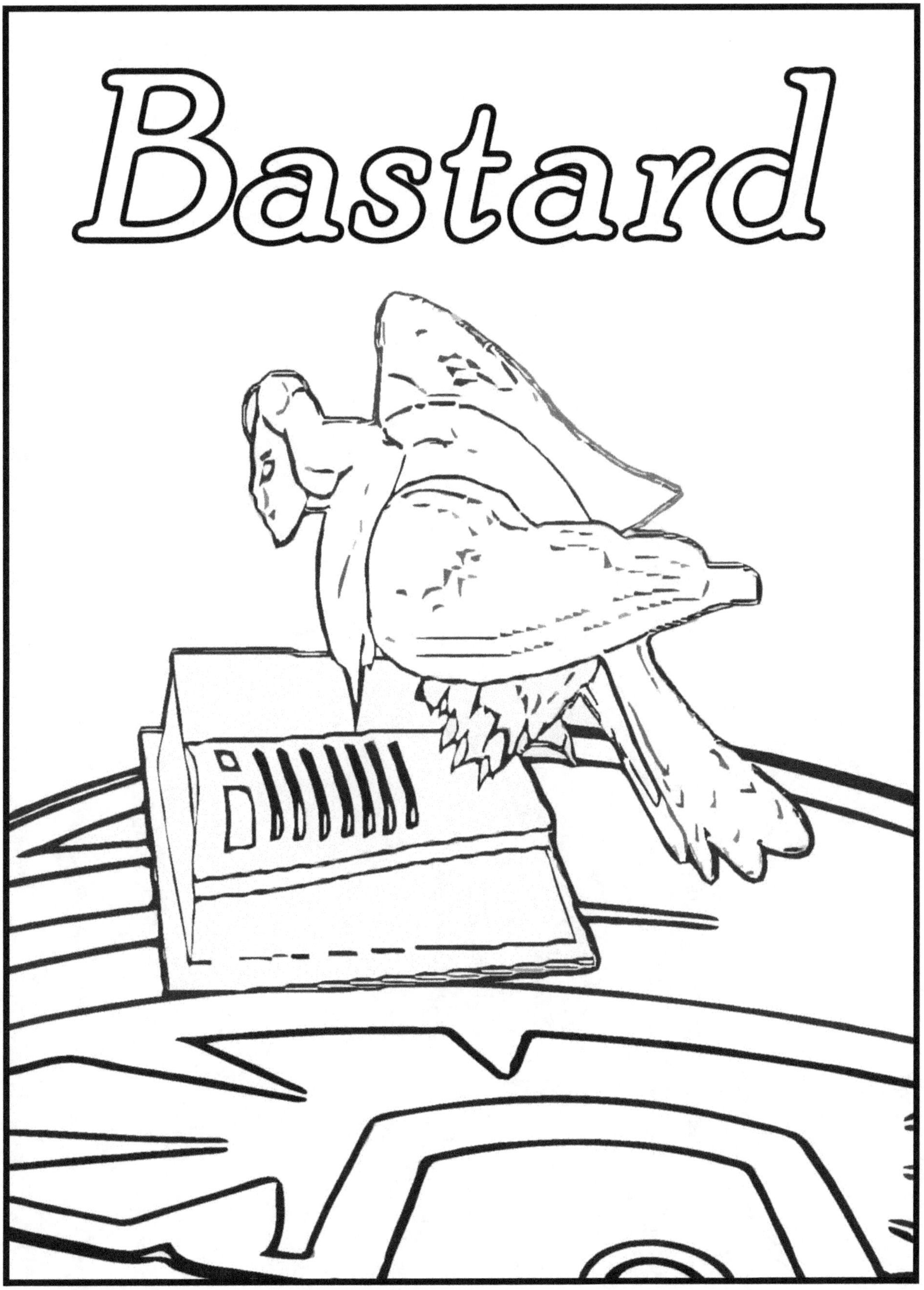
Bastard

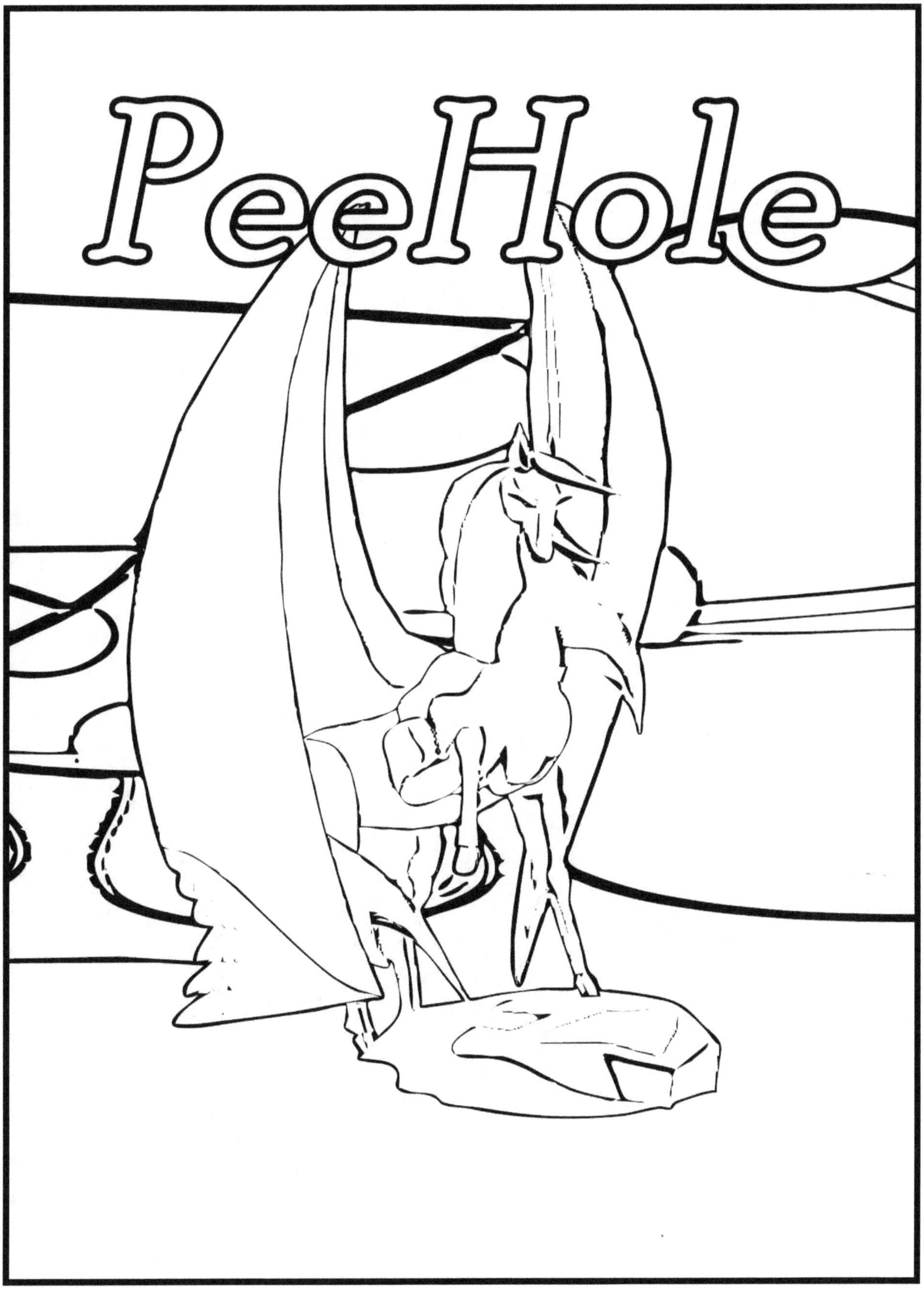
PeeHole

www.ingramcontent.com/pod-product-compliance
Lightning Source LLC
Chambersburg PA
CBHW080614190526
45169CB00007B/3015
9781530152551